Dear God, Where's My Cut?

Dispelling the Lies and Unraveling the Truth

LaQuetta Holyfield Glaze

Dear God: Where is My Cut? Dispelling the Lies and Unraveling the Truth
By: LaQuetta Holyfield Glaze
Copyright © 2018 by LaQuetta Glaze

Cover: Antone Malone, A. Malone Design, LLC
Editing Services: Christian Cashelle, Dynamic Image Publications
Printed in the United States of America.

All rights reserved solely by the author. The author guarantees all contents are original and do not infringe upon the legal rights of any other person or work. No part of this book may be reproduced in any form without the permission of the author. Unless otherwise indicated, Scripture quotations taken from the King James Version (KJV) – public domain

Truth Destinations

Acknowledgments --5
Introduction --9
My Story ---13
Covenants --17
Tithing Horror Stories ---23
Dispelling the Myths of Tithing --29
A Journey Through the Scriptures: A Study Guide ----------------------------39
My Story Part II ---67
A Prophetic Word: For Those Who Have an Ear to Hear ------------------------69
The Path Forward (New Testament Covenant) ----------------------------------71
A Sneak Peak: The Kingdom Strategy of God ----------------------------------81
References ---85
Connecting with LaQuetta ---86

Acknowledgments

The Holy Spirit is my most consistent friend and guide. He is often misunderstood, disrespected, and disregarded. However, if you let Him enter your life, it will never be the same. Every ounce of this book has the imprint of the Holy Spirit.

This book coming to fruition is mostly due to the prayers of some beautiful people. However, there is one that I would like to specifically mention; Dora L. Holyfield, my paternal grandmother. Her prayers throughout my life have kept me from hurt, harm, and danger. She recently departed this earth, but the wisdom that she left me will touch whomever I encounter. She always believed in me, even when I did not believe in myself. She took great care to encourage me in my gifts. I would not be who I am without her. I am a part of her legacy.

To Terrey and my children, Terance and Faith: You all are my love, my light, and my inspiration. Your encouragement is priceless. Your belief in me is strengthening. You all are my very first beta readers. Your love for me is tangible without words, present when you are not around, and proven when the need arises. I love you all to life for life.

Sabrina Price: Honorable. Loving. Kind. A faithful warrior. A supportive friend. A powerful prophet. I appreciate you beyond words. Thank you for your prayers, your encouragement, your protection, and all of your support. I love you. I treasure you and cannot wait to see the things that you will do with God!

Camille Malone: Thanks for challenging my process with your questions. I appreciate you for listening to me, trusting the God in me, teaching me, protecting me, and learning from me. You are the best unofficial research partner! I love you.

Tasha Walker: You have walked with me since forever. I cherish you. I honor you. I love you. Thanks for always believing in me, for teaching me, for learning from me, protecting me, and loving me no matter what. You are the gift in my life and our friendship is a time-honored precious and irreplaceable gift.

Diedra Harris: Your encouragement and contributions have meant the world to me! Your supernatural insight has been invaluable and you have helped to make the crooked places straight. You have my sincerest gratitude.

Tonya Nooks: Thank you for your consistent prayers, biblical insight, your encouragement, protecting me, and for walking me through this journey from the beginning. It has made all of the difference. Thank you for confirming and affirming me.

Antone and Camille Malone: Thank you for your gifts and blessings to me. Your contribution to our lives made this process easier. I honor and treasure you today and always.

Cheryl Eberhardt-Starks: You have been a Godsend in my life. Your prayers, your insight, and your role in my life as a teacher have been monumental. Thank you for your insight as I wrote this book and your encouragement every step of the way.

Introduction

Every Sunday, there are churches all over America narrating that tithes are a requirement for believers of Jesus Christ. Unfortunately, many are doing this under the guise that they have to manipulate believers to give so that they can be blessed. This fallacy must be uncovered and addressed if we expect to move in the higher areas of God.

The church presents tithing as if it is a type of insurance to ensure that the blessing continues to be ours. However, the process really left me asking, "God, where is my cut then?" Where is the return on investment if we are supposed to give to get? Many use tithing as an insurance policy or an investment strategy. In the secular community, insurance is paid and investments are made because one wants a reliable, predictable, and guarantee-controllable outcome. Marketing tithing as a return on investment strategy is not God's way, it completely negates our Kingdom roles, rights, and responsibilities. His love, power, and protection do not have to be earned; these belong to us as Kingdom heirs.

Giving to receive was never God's way, even for those who tithed. Giving should be about love, honor, and obedience to God. While giving me the assignment to write this book, the Lord said this is the time that He will begin to dispel lies in the Body of Christ. The time for guilty giving has expired. The receipt of money from people who are not even in a position to give has expired as well.

This book will be part of a series and will cover an in-depth look at the Scriptures that speak about tithing and the position of Jesus. It is time for the Body of Christ to transition from borrower to lender. We are to perform our roles as the change agent of the world that God has called us to be.

This book's purpose is to be a source of hope and a catalyst for change for those who are eager to follow the word of the Lord indeed. The key focus of this book is to dispel the lie. It is also to help understand there is a more excellent way; we should give because we love Him.

Let's get started, shall we?

My Story

For most of my life, I believed in tithing. Every teacher, pastor, elder, and leader emphasized its importance. Tithing was taught as the holy thing to do. There was not a Sunday that did not contain a reminder that tithes and offerings support the ministers of the Gospel, tangible items such as utilities, church mortgages, and insurance, and to further the spread of the Good News. Money is an essential asset in any organization, that part is correct. Believers should want to participate in giving – especially since God mandates it, right?

Hearing about the benefits of tithing was so refreshing. I mean who wouldn't want the great blessing one did not have room enough to receive? I used to imagine looking around rooms that were filled with blessings that overflowed into other rooms. I used to be afraid that I would be "cursed with a curse" if I did not give my full tithe. I chalked up my inner voice to sin, greed, and unrighteousness.

Nevertheless, deep down I still had questions. I had concerns. Malachi 3:10 haunted me like Freddy Kruger in folks' nightmares. Yet, I tried to overcome that by continuing to give and encouraging others that the principle was sound.

One Sunday still stands out vividly. That particular Sunday was my day to handle the tithes and offerings. I had a compelling story to share with the congregation on this very matter. The previous week, I struggled with paying my tithes because we had some other financial responsibilities piling up. So, I tore up the check and used those funds to pay what we needed. However, the refrigerator began to make this terrible noise that sounded like it was breaking down. Terrified of the fridge breaking down, I began to rewrite the check for the tithes and interestingly enough, the refrigerator started to hum normally. After activating my "extra holiness" superpower (queue the Superman theme music), I chalked this up to the fact that I was breaking the curse by choosing to pay my tithes. I used this story to encourage others to tithe and to keep God's protection in their lives by tithing. I was wrong.

In 2009, my family moved to a different state. When we arrived, one of the first things God told me was that He was going to deprogram me. It was a time to question everything that I thought I knew and leave no stone unturned. It was at this point that I heard God say that we were to stop tithing. I was so scared.

"But I'll go to hell," I told God. Interestingly enough, I didn't receive a reply.

Understand that at this point in my walk with God, I was not considered a novice. I was confident in discerning whether it was my voice, God's voice, or the enemy's voice. Not only that, but it was at this point where I was a trusted prophet in many people's lives as well as a confidant and woman of counsel. This situation could not be chalked up to a misunderstanding, but that is precisely what I did – chalked it up to a mistake.

When God wants me to do something, I cannot shake it until it has been completed. It is not like ducking from lightning. The task echoes in me until it is done. The frequency varies, but it stays with me until I move. I believe that the timing was necessary because a year or two before this command, that beam in my eye would have blocked me from even hearing that word. I consulted with some men and women of God upon first receipt of the prophetic word. A few confirmed that I had heard God correctly and a few told me that I missed it. To be honest with you, I hoped I had missed it, because I knew that this would be life-changing for me and that all of that change would not feel good.

So, I decided to trust that I heard God correctly and stop tithing. Not too long after I reluctantly relented to God's word, I received a 20% pay increase at work and two bonuses within 18 months. This type of pay raise was unprecedented on any job, especially the kind of job I had at the time.

From 2009 to 2015, there was a lot of praying, studying, and researching. I had a lot of questions as many of you do. God took the time to answer every one. What began to happen in 2016 changed my life. Take the journey with me through what's next and I'll finish my story later in the book.

Covenants

To conceptually understand the Bible and the applicability of tithing, one has to understand God's covenants. A covenant is a clause that governs essential relationships. Covenants are solemn, binding declarations that give effect to promises. The terms of the new contract secures the promise of **eternal redemption.** There are three types of covenants, but this book will focus on divine covenants with the definitions listed below.

Divine Covenants

Divine covenants are the promises God made with man. The divine covenant is the type of promise that applies to tithing. The most important item to remember about a covenant is the WHAT and the WHO that will be covered under the bond.

Here are some of the covenants covered in the Bible:

Adamic Covenant: This is the outline of man's responsibility for creation. This covenant includes God's command regarding the tree of the knowledge of good and evil, the curses for the sin of Adam and Eve, as well as God's provision for that sin.

(Scripture reference: Genesis 3:15)

Noahic Covenant: This is a promise between Noah and God, but extends to humanity overall. The Noahic contract is the promise that God would never destroy all life on earth with a flood. The promise was sealed with a rainbow visible after rain. (**Scripture reference: Genesis 9**)

Abrahamic Covenant: God's promise to Abraham was plenteous. God promised to make his name great. God promised that Abraham would have numerous physical descendants; he would be father to a multitude of nations and that families of the world would be blessed through his blood line. The Abrahamic contract was a reference to the Messiah, Jesus Christ. (**Scripture references: Genesis 12, 13, 15, and 17**)

Mosaic Covenant: The Mosaic covenant was one of condition, meaning that the outcome was based on the action of its participants. It was based solely on Israel's ability to obey the commands of God. It includes the Ten Commandments and the law. There are 613 laws. The Old Testament is full of chronicles that outline their success and failures of obeying the law. **(Scripture references: Deuteronomy 11)**

Covenant of Levi/Priestly Covenant: The tribe of Levi was God's designated priests and descendants of Aaron. The Levites was the only tribe that was not allowed to own land. Therefore, the promise that the tribe of Levi received was a portion of the holy things dedicated to God's tabernacle. This is a promise within a covenant; it is a promise to the Levites for honoring the Mosaic laws. **(Scripture references: Exodus 40:15, Leviticus 2:13, Numbers 18:19, Jeremiah 33:21)**

Davidic Covenant: God promised that David's lineage would last forever and that his kingdom would never pass. This promise is honored through the fact that Jesus is the King. **(Scripture references: 2 Samuel 7:8-16, Luke 1:32-33)**

New Covenant: The New Covenant is a one for all humanity. Jesus Christ came to fulfill the Law of Moses and create a new covenant between God and His people. All 613 laws are translated into one command: *Love thy neighbor as thyself.* All people – Jews and Gentiles can be free from the Law. Kingdom rights belong to all as a gift from God based on the sacrifice that Jesus made with His blood, His life, and His resurrection. (**Scripture references: Jeremiah 31:34, Matthew 5:17, Ephesians 2:8-9**)

Tithing Horror Stories

Here are some real life stories and church situations to show the devastation that tithing can bring:

- *When this church started, it had 10 people including my family. Early on, I would always give an offering from my heart. As we grew in leadership, we would have classes on Malachi 3:10. The words etched in my head were, 'Will a man rob God' and 'You are cursed with a curse.' I tithed faithfully even when I had to decide how much I needed to cut the grocery bill, gas in the car, or even household items. One day, I received a disconnect notice on my lights. I would not get paid until two days after the date and they would not make arrangements with me. So, I called the church. The cutoff was 5 p.m. and I was at work. I called the pastor and he said I had to come to the church. I left work around 10 that morning and went to the church. I was told that I had to fill out an application to request money from the church and it would have to go before the finance board. I filled it out and was then told they would call me. I got the call around 3:30 p.m. to come back to the church to meet with the board. They sat me at a table with three members in front of me, interview style, as they looked over my application. I had to explain my income and expenses, including groceries. All of the members asked questions. I faithfully paid my tithes and when I was on the finance board I did not recall giving other members this much grief. By the time they finished with me, I was so hurt. They finally told me that they would give me the money, but it was a loan. I had to agree to a scheduled repayment agreement in addition to my tithes. I could not miss paying my tithes or the loan. Any piece of dignity was shredded at that moment. If I am faithful in doing right in God's eyes, why am I being punished for it? The following Sunday, the pastor preached yet another sermon with my name on it.*

- *Prayer Line Craziness: There was a prominent preacher who served as the invited speaker. He was responsible for the "exhortation" during the giving time. He began to speak about giving and then stated that God told him to pray a special prayer of blessing for a specific high-dollar amount. During a popular conference the doors were blocked and no one was "allowed" to go out during giving time. The reason given for having the ushers stand in front of the door was to ensure that the flow of the service continued and everyone heard the call to give. This is not biblical. What's even crazier is that the line was long to give in order to receive a special prayer of favor with God. As believers, God loves us all equally and we do not need to give to obtain favor from Him. We need to heed the commandments that He gives as we are led by the Holy Spirit.*

- There are quite a few churches that require individuals to submit their W-2s as a qualification for leadership in the church. Other churches have hired full-time employees and required them to submit to an automatic 10% deduction from their paychecks or the job offer is nullified.

- There is a story where a prominent boxer believed that he should give 10% of his income when presented with a choice between paying his tithe or his mortgage. The property foreclosed.

- There are instances where churches ask members to obtain loans and refinance/mortgage their homes to "support the mission" with promise of repayment. The churches have shut down, filed bankruptcy, or otherwise never reconciled their debts to those who gave in faith. This caused ripples of debt and devastation that would take years to overcome. Retired folks had to take on new jobs to recover. Some folks filed for bankruptcy. Others recovered, but it took years to overcome.

These instances are manipulations, lies, and the downright hustling of the people of God. By using the name of God, twisting the scripture, and taking advantage of people's trust and vulnerability, a lot of pain was inflicted in the one place that people should feel safe, which is in the house of God.

Tithing was never meant for a person to give so that they can get a car, house, or other valuables. It was never meant as a means to get what you want from God.

Dispelling the Myths of Tithing

There are a lot of myths where tithing is concerned. Let's walk through them together (listed in no certain order).

Myth: Every single promise in the bible is applicable for every single person.

Truth: God operates in covenants (promises). The covenant that requires tithing is the Mosaic covenant designed for the Israelites. Remember that a covenant is so much more than a promise. Covenants are solemn, binding declarations that give effect to promises and govern important relationships.

Myth: Tithing was mandated for everyone even before the law of Moses.

Truth: Abraham tithed one time and it was to Melchizedek. It was not from his wealth, but the spoils of war. There are no other indicated times of tithing from Abraham and most importantly, no indication that God required that. This passage of scripture is known as "the first tithe." Yes, it is the first recorded tithe. Abraham used it as a response to God's blessing. He already had God's blessing. We all have God's blessing and do not have to give in response to His blessing.

We are to give cheerfully for the betterment of the Kingdom and as led by the Holy Spirit. Abraham was already wealthy and only gave out of the increase from the spoils of war.

Jacob's tenth was a tenth of increase and not a requirement. Jacob offered because he loved God and His faithfulness. The 613 Old Testament laws included tithing. James 2:10 states, "For whosoever shall keep the whole law, and yet offend in one point, he is ***guilty*** of all." If you tithe, you are required to follow the law in its entirety or be found guilty of all.

Tithing was a Jewish practice that was primarily used to support people in need and was not practiced outside the land of Israel (Blizzard, p. 40).

Myth: God was speaking to all people in Malachi 3:8-10, one of the most utilized scriptures to support tithing.

Truth: In Malachi 3:8-10, God reprimands Israel by reiterating the blessings and curses placed under that covenant. God is speaking to leadership because they are the ones who have access to the tithe.

Myth: The tithe was always money.

Truth: The tithe was a ***tenth of the increase*** of one's income. Some people may have worked, but there was no increase to generate the ability to give. The tithe was not money; it was food, oil, wine, etc. (Deuteronomy 14:22-27). When the tithe could not be carried to the tent of meeting it was exchanged for money, but there were rules. The money was to be bound in hand, the person had to go to the place God designated, buy whatever their heart desired, eat and celebrate the Lord and not forget about the Levites in their town.

Myth: First fruit offerings are required to be blessed in the Kingdom.

Truth: The first fruit offering had a specific intent and there is no evidence it was to be a part of any giving strategy for the Body of Christ. The first fruits were a part of the Mosaic covenant requirement and included dough, offerings, the fruit from all kinds of trees, the new wine, and oil (Nehemiah 10:37-38). It is associated with giving God thanks for the journey from Egypt to Canaan. There is no biblical precedent that requires New Testament believers to participate in a first fruit offering. Jesus is the first fruit of the current covenant (Romans 8:23, John 14:26, 1 Corinthians 15:20, 23). The New Testament saints are considered the first fruits of the covenant (2 Thessalonians 2:13 and James 1:18).

The tithe was set aside for the Levites who were restricted from owning anything as the ministers of God. Today, every believer of Jesus Christ is a part of the royal priesthood. 1 Peter 2:9 states, "But ye are a chosen generation, a royal priesthood, a holy generation, a peculiar people (special/ set apart); that ye should shew forth the praises of Him who hath called you out of darkness into His marvelous light." We are all set aside and have the responsibility of the final commandment of Jesus which was, "Go ye therefore and teach all nations, baptizing them in the name of the Father, and of the Son, and of the Holy Ghost." If a person cannot trace their lineage back to the tribe of Levi, the ones who are receiving tithes are in grave error and sin.

Myth: Current believers are required to tithe today.

Truth: Jesus, Peter, and Paul did NOT receive the tithe. Jesus was a descendant of the tribe of Judah (Matthew 1:1-6 and Luke 3:31-34). A great majority of Paul's teachings were dedicated to showing us that we are not under the law or any type of work righteousness. In Galatians 4:9,

Paul describes life under the Old Testament as weak and beggarly bondage: "But now, after that ye have known God, or rather are known of God, how turn ye again to the weak and beggarly elements, whereunto ye desire again to be in bondage?"

Myth: New Testament believers are cursed if they do not tithe.

Truth: New Testament believers are not cursed if they do not tithe. Believers should not assume that they have to give to get the very things that are theirs by birthright! God is not sitting on His throne waiting to smack a curse on a person's entire life if they pay their electrical bill instead of tithing. There is no such thing as God insurance. God insurance is a payment to ensure that you are good with God and your life is covered. Jesus already took care of that at the cross and resurrection. We were assured long before we were here! Glory!

A Journey Through the Scriptures: A Study Guide

(King James Version)

Listed below are scriptures in the Old and New Testament that discuss tithing. All tithing scriptures fall under the Mosaic covenant, except for Abraham and Jacob's example. The purpose of this section is for independent study. It is the responsibility of each believer to understand the scriptures and the context of each scripture to be effective witnesses for Christ. Let the Holy Spirit be your guide and your friend as you navigate through this section.

Genesis 14:20 – "And blessed be the most high God, which hath delivered thine enemies into thy hand. And he gave him tithes of all."

Scriptural Context: In this bible verse, Melchizedek comes out to meet

Abraham as Abraham gives him a tithe of the spoils of his victory.

Genesis 28:20-22 – "And Jacob vowed a vow, saying, If God will be with me, and will keep me in this way that I go, and will give me bread to eat, and raiment to put on, So that I come to my father's house in peace; then shall the Lord be my God: And this stone, which I have set for a pillar, shall be God's house: and of all that thou shalt give me I will surely give a tenth unto thee."

Scriptural Context: After the vision of God's renewed covenant, Jacob initiates a covenant with God, vowing to give him a tithe of what he receives from the Promised Land.

Leviticus 27:30-32 – "And all the tithe of the land, whether of the seed of the land, or of the fruit of the tree, is the Lord's: it is holy unto the Lord. And if a man will at all to redeem ought of his tithes, he shall add thereto the fifth part thereof. And concerning the tithe of the herd, or of the flock, event of whatever passeth under the rod, the tenth shall be holy unto the Lord."

Scriptural Context: The specifications of tithing are introduced into the law of Moses.

Numbers 18:20-32 – "And the Lord spake unto Aaron, Thou shall have no inheritance in their land, neither shalt thou have any part among them: I am thy part and thine inheritance among the children of Israel. And, behold, I have given the children of Levi all the tenth in Israel for an inheritance, for their service which they serve, even the service of the tabernacle of the congregation. Neither must the children of Israel henceforth come nigh the tabernacle of the congregation, lest they bear sin, and die. But the Levites shall do the service of the tabernacle of the congregation, and they shall bear their iniquity: it shall be a statute forever throughout your generations, that among the children of Israel they have no inheritance. But the tithes of the children of Israel, which they offer as an heave offering unto the Lord, I have given to the Levites to inherit: therefore I have said unto them, Among the children of Israel they shall have no inheritance. And the Lord spake unto Moses, saying, Thus speak unto the Levites, and say to them, When ye take of the children of Israel the tithes which I have given you from them for your inheritance, then ye shall offer up an heave offering of it for the Lord, even a tenth part of the tithe. And this your heave offering shall be reckoned unto you, as though it were the corn of the threshing floor, and as the fulness of the winepress. Thus ye also shall offer an heave offering unto the Lord of all your tithes, which ye receive of the children of Israel; and ye shall give thereof the Lord's heave offering to Aaron the priest. Out of all your gifts ye shall offer every heave offering of the Lord, of all the best thereof, even the hallowed part thereof out of it. Therefore thou shalt say until them, When ye have heaved the best thereof from it, then it shall be counted unto the Levites as the increase of the threshing floor, and as the increase of the winepress. And ye shall eat it in every place, ye and your households:

for it is your reward for your service in the tabernacle of the congregation. And ye shall bear no sin by reason of it, when ye have heaved from it the best of it: neither shall ye pollute the holy things of the children of Israel, lest ye die.

Scriptural Context: The Terumah (Hebrew: תְּרוּמָה), plural Terumot, is a heave offering. The word is used in the positive sense of presenting an offering to God. A *heave* is a simple upward movement. It could speak to heaving the sacrifice toward the altar or it could refer to separating a portion of the sacrifice from the rest. The Levites were not given an inheritance like the other tribes; God stated that

He was their portion and inheritance amongst the children of Israel for the work that they do in the tabernacle.

Deuteronomy 12:5-11 – "But unto the place which the Lord your God shall choose out of all your tribes to put his name there, even unto his habitation shall ye seek, and thither thou shalt come: And thither ye shall bring your burnt offerings, and your sacrifices, and your tithes, and heave offerings of your hand, and your vows, and your freewill offerings, and the firstlings of your herds and of your flocks: And there ye shall eat before the Lord your God, and ye shall rejoice in all that ye put your hand unto, ye

and your households, wherein
the Lord thy God hath blessed thee. Ye
shall not do after all the things that we
do here this day, every man
whatsoever is right in his own eyes.
For ye are not as yet come to the rest
and to the inheritance, which
the Lord your God giveth you. But
when ye go over Jordan, and dwell in
the land which the Lord your God
giveth you to inherit, and when he
giveth you rest from all your enemies
round about, so that ye dwell in safety;
Then there shall be a place which
the Lord your God shall choose to
cause his name to dwell there; thither
shall ye bring all that I command you;
your burnt offerings, and your

sacrifices, your tithes, and the heave offering of your hand, and all your choice vows which ye vow unto the Lord:

Scriptural Context: God gives instructions for what to do with the tithe once Israel crosses the Jordan (the Promised Land).

Deuteronomy 14:22-29 – "Thou shalt truly tithe all the increase of thy seed, that the field bringeth forth year by year. And thou shalt eat before the Lord thy God, in the place which he shall choose to place his name there, the tithe of thy corn, of thy wine, and of thine oil, and the firstlings of thy herds and of thy flocks; that thou

Dear God, Where's My Cut?

mayest learn to fear the Lord thy God always. And if the way be too long for thee, so that thou art not able to carry it; or if the place be too far from thee, which the Lord thy God shall choose to set his name there, when the Lord thy God hath blessed thee: Then shalt thou turn it into money, and bind up the money in thine hand, and shalt go unto the place which the Lord thy God shall choose: And thou shalt bestow that money for whatsoever thy soul lusteth after, for oxen, or for sheep, or for wine, or for strong drink, or for whatsoever thy soul desireth: and thou shalt eat there before the Lord thy God, and thou shalt rejoice, thou, and thine household, And the Levite that is within thy gates; thou shalt not forsake him; for he hath no part nor inheritance with thee. At the end of three years thou shalt bring forth all the tithe of thine increase the same year, and shalt lay it up within thy gates: And the Levite, (because he hath no part nor inheritance with thee,) and the stranger, and the fatherless, and the widow, which are within thy gates, shall come, and shall eat and be satisfied; that the Lord thy God may bless thee in all the work of thine hand which thou doest.

Scriptural Context: God gives instructions on how to disperse and exchange the tithe. These included directions for the third year, which is a tithe for the stranger, the widow, and the fatherless amongst them.

Deuteronomy 26:12-15 – "When thou hast made an end of tithing all the tithes of thine increase the third year, which is the year of tithing, and hast given it unto the Levite, the stranger, the fatherless, and the widow, that they may eat within thy gates, and be filled; Then thou shalt say before the Lord thy God, I have brought away the hallowed things out of mine house, and also have given them unto the Levite, and unto the stranger, to the fatherless, and to the widow, according to all thy commandments which thou hast commanded me: I have not transgressed thy commandments, neither have I forgotten them: I have not eaten thereof in my mourning, neither have I taken away ought thereof for any unclean use, nor given ought thereof for the dead: but I have hearkened to the voice of the Lord my God, and have done according to all that thou hast commanded me. Look down from thy holy habitation, from heaven, and bless thy people Israel, and the land which thou hast given us, as thou swarest unto our fathers, a land that floweth with milk and honey.

Scriptural Context: God gives instructions on how Israel should sanctify the tithe before they can ask for a blessing.

2 Chronicles 31:5-12 – "And as soon as the commandment came abroad, the children of Israel brought in abundance the first fruits of corn, wine, and oil, and honey, and of all the increase of the field; and the tithe of all things brought they in abundantly. And concerning the children of Israel and Judah, that dwelt in the cities of Judah, they also brought in the tithe of oxen and sheep, and the tithe of holy things which were consecrated unto the Lord their God, and laid them by heaps. In the third month they began to lay the foundation of the heaps, and finished them in the seventh month. And when Hezekiah and the princes came and saw the heaps, they blessed the Lord, and his people Israel. Then Hezekiah questioned with the priests and the Levites concerning the heaps. And Azariah the chief priest of the house of Zadok answered him, and said, Since the people began to bring the offerings into the house of the Lord, we have had enough to eat, and have left plenty: for the Lord hath blessed his people; and that which is left is this great store. Then Hezekiah commanded to prepare chambers in the house of the Lord; and they prepared them, And brought in the offerings and the tithes and the dedicated things faithfully: over which Cononiah the Levite was ruler, and Shimei his brother was the next."

Scriptural Context: The children of Israel do what is right under Hezekiah's reign and bring the tithes to the designated places. Israel is blessed for their obedience to God's commandments.

Nehemiah 10:37-38 – "And that we should bring the first fruits of our dough, and our offerings, and the fruit of all manner of trees, of wine and of oil, unto the priests, to the chambers of the house of our God; and the tithes of our ground unto the Levites, that the same Levites might have the tithes in all the cities of our tillage. And the priest the son of Aaron shall be with the Levites, when the Levites take tithes: and the Levites shall bring up the tithe of the tithes unto the house of our God, to the chambers, into the treasure house."

Scriptural Context: Israel obeys God and brings the tithes and first fruit offering to the storehouse.

Nehemiah 12:44 – "And at that time were some appointed over the chambers for the treasures, for the offerings, for the first fruits, and for the tithes, to gather into them out of the fields of the cities the portions of the law for the priests and Levites: for

Judah rejoiced for the priests and for the Levites that waited."

Scriptural Context: Officers were appointed to watch over the tithes in the storehouse.

Nehemiah 13:5-12 – "And he had prepared for him a great chamber, where aforetime they laid the meat offerings, the frankincense, and the vessels, and the tithes of the corn, the new wine, and the oil, which was commanded to be given to the Levites, and the singers, and the porters; and the offerings of the priests. But in all this time was not I at Jerusalem: for in the two and thirtieth year of Artaxerxes king of Babylon came I unto the king,

and after certain days obtained I leave
of the king: And I came to Jerusalem,
and understood of the evil that Eliashib
did for Tobiah, in preparing him a
chamber in the courts of the house of
God. And it grieved me sore: therefore
I cast forth all the household stuff of
Tobiah out of the chamber. Then I
commanded, and they cleansed the
chambers: and thither brought I again
the vessels of the house of God, with
the meat offering and the frankincense.
And I perceived that the portions of
the Levites had not been given them:
for the Levites and the singers, that did
the work, were fled every one to his
field. Then contended I with the rulers,
and said, Why is the house of God

forsaken? And I gathered them together, and set them in their place. Then brought all Judah the tithe of the corn and the new wine and the oil unto the treasuries."

Scriptural Context: Nehemiah cleanses the storehouse and kicks Tobiah out of the room designated to store the tithe. He then restores order.

<u>Amos 4:4</u> – "Come to Beth–el, and transgress; at Gilgal multiply transgression; and bring your sacrifices every morning, and your tithes after three years:"

Scriptural Context: God commands Israel to bring back the tithe and reiterates the consequences (calamities; discussed further in the chapter) that will fall upon them if they don't.

Malachi 3:8-10 – "Will a man rob God? Yet ye have robbed me. But ye say, Wherein have we robbed thee? In tithes and offerings. Ye are cursed with a curse: for ye have robbed me, even this whole nation. Bring ye all the tithes into the storehouse, that there may be meat in mine house, and prove me now herewith, saith the Lord of hosts, if I will not open you the windows of heaven, and pour you out a blessing, that there shall not be room enough to receive it."

Scriptural Context: God reprimands Israel for not delivering the tithe and reiterates the blessings and curses that would result from whatever decision they chose. Note: In one of my first experiences with God concerning tithing, He spoke to me and said that this scripture was not speaking to the people; He was speaking to leadership and in this case- those who are collecting the tithes.

Matthew 23:23 – "Woe unto you, scribes and Pharisees, hypocrites! for ye pay tithe of mint and anise and cummin, and have omitted the weightier matters of the law, judgment, mercy, and faith: these ought ye to have done, and not to leave the other undone.

Scriptural Context: Jesus rebukes the Pharisees for not obeying the weightier matters of the law and tithing. Jesus wants them to focus on more important matters and not their list. Their priorities are not in order.

Luke 11:42 – "But woe unto you, Pharisees! for ye tithe mint and rue and all manner of herbs, and pass over judgment and the love of God: these ought ye to have done, and not to leave the other undone."

Scriptural Context: A parallel Bible verse of Matthew 23:23; as Jesus rebukes the Pharisees for not obeying the weightier matters of the law along with tithing.

Luke 18:12 – "I fast twice in the week, I give tithes of all that I possess."

Scriptural Context: A Pharisee brags about his obedience to the law and tithing.

Hebrews 7:5-22 – "And verily they that are of the sons of Levi, who receive the office of the priesthood, have a commandment to take tithes of the people according to the law, that is, of their brethren, though they come out of the loins of Abraham: But he whose descent is not counted from them received tithes of Abraham, and blessed him that had the promises. And without all contradiction the less is blessed of the better. And here men that die receive tithes; but there he receiveth them, of whom it is witnessed that he liveth. And as I may so say, Levi also, who receiveth tithes, payed tithes in Abraham. For he was yet in the loins of his father, when Melchisedec met him. If therefore perfection were by the Levitical priesthood, (for under it the people received the law,) what further need was there that another priest should rise after the order of Melchisedec, and not be called after the order of Aaron? For the priesthood being changed, there is made of necessity a change also of the law. For he of whom these things are spoken pertaineth to another tribe, of which no man gave attendance at the altar. For it is evident that our Lord sprang out of Judah; of which tribe Moses spake nothing concerning priesthood. And it is yet far more evident: for that after the similitude of Melchisedec there ariseth another priest, Who is made, not after the law of a carnal commandment, but after the power of an endless life. For he testifieth, Thou art a priest for ever after the order of Melchisedec. For there is verily a disannulling of the commandment going before for the weakness and unprofitableness thereof.

For the law made nothing perfect, but the bringing in of a better hope did; by the which we draw nigh unto God. And inasmuch as not without an oath he was made priest: (For those priests were made without an oath; but this with an oath by him that said unto him, The Lord sware and will not repent, Thou art a priest for ever after the order of Melchisedec:) By so much was Jesus made a surety of a better testament."

Scriptural Context: Abraham's tithe is used to illustrate a change from the Levitical priesthood to the priesthood and covenant of Christ.

My Story Part II

As you recall, there is a story about me persuading people to tithe based on the purr of a refrigerator. I asked God why the refrigerator began to hum normally again after I rewrote the check. He said that it was the spirit of religion that blinded me to only what it wanted me to see. He said that He was not cursing me by making me think that I would have to sink the money into the refrigerator. The enemy of our soul uses the spirit and ritual of religion to keep people blind to their covenant freedom by covering the truth. He said that the sacrifice of Jesus covered it all and is not contingent on my giving. Provision is a part of the package. We could never give enough to recompense for what has been given to us anyway.

Let's pick up where we left off; the arrival of our family in Florida. After many years of praying, having dreams, and receiving confirmations, I resigned from my Memphis position and moved into the unknown through obedience. In the first days of 2016, God began with a word for the people of God for me to release. The word that the Lord spoke was this: I will begin to dispel the lies in the Body of Christ.

In my mind, I was like, *Yes, God! Do it, God!* That was until I heard what my specific assignment was. It was to write this book. I felt a sense of excitement and trembled at what I knew was coming. What was coming is what comes for all of us; especially leaders in the Body of Christ: I had to walk through the journey of life to be an example and a life cheat code for someone else. A life cheat code is the sharing of a specific journey where a person can experience victory for the specific purpose of moving forward without the delay of the experience. If we have traveled down a road and know that it has a pothole, we should share that experience so that others can learn from it and have a smoother ride. We have had financial travesties while tithing and not tithing. We have had increases on both sides as well.

We have lost some material items and had to wait on a lot of things. However, God never said that we would never experience the downside of life; rain falls on the just and the unjust. He said that He would be with us through it all. However, I will tell you that I have experienced more miracles, signs, and wonders while walking in the fullness of His covenant. We have less overall income, but we are not lacking anything in our lives. We have had the potential of major losses come closer than we would have liked, but we made it through. We have had favor where we should not have had favor. We have had our groceries randomly paid for when we were low on funds and we have had bills dramatically decreased, just to name a few. These are hard things to need and receive when you are normally the one doing the giving. Through it all, God has shown us that harkening to His voice will never lead us astray.

A Prophetic Word: For Those Who Have an Ear to Hear

As I went through this process, I asked God to confirm that this was the right path despite life's ups and downs.

Thus says the Lord:

"Tithing has been winked at for the sake of growth and maturity. However, the grace for living under the lies of tithing will soon cease. There will be a distinguishable difference in those who obey My word concerning giving and those who disregard My warning."

The word *winked* is used in Acts 17:30 and is a confirmation of this prophetic word. Acts 17:30 states, "And the times of this ignorance God winked at; but now commandeth all men everywhere to repent:" As always, it is important to note that grace is always with us and will abound, but it is time for growth to be abound as well.

The Path Forward (New Testament Covenant)

A few key reminders:

- Tithing is under the Mosaic covenant.
- Tithing is one of 613 laws.
- First fruit offerings are a part of the Mosaic covenant.
- James 2:10 tells us that one has to follow all of the laws or be guilty of them all.
- Jesus fulfilled the law when He died and rose. All 613 laws. He did not leave one out because He didn't have a plan to finance the church.

Although the purpose of this book is to correct and dispel the lie of tithing for believers today, I could not release the book without talking about giving and its relevance to the Body of Christ. Jesus nor any of the New Testament writers neither affirmed or confirmed that tithing was a requirement under the new covenant. Matthew

5:17 states, "Think not that I am come to destroy the law, or the prophets: I am not come to destroy, but to fulfil."

A lot of people seem to think this means that Jesus would destroy or cancel the law. He did not. He fulfilled it and granted our liberty with His death. To fulfill something means to complete it. According to the dictionary, fulfill is derived from the Old English word fullyllan, meaning "fill up or make full." The dictionary definition is to fill full, accomplish, and carry out or to bring to realization, to perform or do, as in a person's duty; or to obey or follow the Commandments, as in completing the Commandments by obeying them. Jesus came to complete the law and fulfill the words of the prophets before Him.

When He completed the law, believers were released into freedom and had access to every Kingdom resource that God has in Heaven. Why would Jesus make His life a sacrifice for every law except for tithing? If that is the case, then why would His sacrifice even be needed? The sacrifice that Jesus made was the final covenant that was needed in the earth. It is perfect and complete. Every believer alive has access to the covenant of Jesus.

Do not confuse laws with conditions. Many would argue that believers have to give in order to get. That is not true. Believers have equal rights to everything in the Kingdom. They do not have to give to obtain God's blessing, His provision, or His love. Those are automatically theirs, forever and always. However, God does require obedience and adherence to His word. Grace and consequences belong to the believer because sowing and reaping is a principle in the Kingdom of God.

The family unit is a parallel to the way God functions with us concerning access, accountability, and responsibility. Children are born into a family; believers are born again into the Kingdom of God. Love, blessing, and approval belong to them forever and always. They will have access to everything that the family has in its possession; the same is also true in the Kingdom of God. Just like in your family, giving money does not guarantee or diminish a believers place in the Kingdom. God does not curse a believer for not giving. When God looks at the believer He sees Jesus, not the tithing record of a believer. Jesus did not tithe/give a tenth of His blood; He gave it all so that we could have it all in Him.

The time for guilty giving and the receipt of money from people who are not even in a position to give has ended. The time for financial manipulation in the church has ended. It is time to get on track with God's plan. To do this we have to surrender our opinion to God's truth. Denominations (root word division), the number of church splits, and the consistent businesslike atmosphere of church versus an atmosphere of love, truth, and acceptance indicates that human opinion is running the church and not His truth.

Many leaders know that the law of tithing is not for today. However, they continue to feed the lie because they do not have the faith that you will give to their vision or the vision of the assembly you are attending. This is a very old lie that has perpetuated throughout the centuries and ties back to the Roman Catholic Church.

"The forced imposition of the tithe upon the Church was the product of a corrupt clergy within the Roman Catholic Church" (Blizzard, 41).

These people believe that it is easier to manipulate the congregation into believing that tithing is required so that they can have a predictable income. The outcome of this behavior results in people struggling to be faithful, wondering if they should tithe or pay their electric bill. This behavior also means that the church leaders lack faith. If God has given a mission, He also provides the provision. That is not a cliché; that is the truth.

The church should be a part of the rebuilding process for its members and not keep them in a cycle of poverty. Yes, some people will not give, that is not for any leader or believer to fix: that is the job of the Holy Spirit. The church cannot continue to say, "Lord, have your way" and then proceed to limit Him by manipulating His children.

The church cannot continue to say, "Trust Him with your finances," yet do not ascribe to that same level of trust with God because it has the steady income of members coming in. The provision of the Body of Christ will come from the Body of Christ, but first the Body of Christ needs to be reset in terms of financial strategy. The bamboozlement, manipulation, and lies have caused a lot of hurt. Healing and reconciliation have to take place to birth the new thing that God is going to do.

The New Testament gives us liberty and freedom through the sacrifice that Christ made with His life.

Believers are to love God with everything. Everything a believer has belongs to God; the full 100% and not just a tenth. If we are in relationship with God, we will seek His guidance first and follow the Holy Spirit's guidance for giving individually. The key to giving is the same key to life as a believer; simply listen and obey. The leaders who teach tithing limit the increase that is needed in the Body of Christ. When a leader requires, demands, and manipulates a believer to only giving 10%, they may be overriding the Holy Spirit. There are plenty of givers that would increase their giving in obedience to the Holy Spirit, but they cannot hear the call because they are only hearing 10% from their leaders. Even if they did hear the call, they may relent and give 10%. Let's face it, 10% sounds a lot better than 40% or 50% and when facing God they can blame His leadership! However, this is not going to last forever.

Every believer is responsible for their own actions. The scripture says that we are to work out our own salvation through fear and trembling; we work together on earth, but we will account for our actions individually. The time is overdue for us to listen to God, seek His face first, and let the Holy Spirit guide every action.

The time has come for the Body of Christ to let go of their personal opinion, perceptions, and feeling to obtain clarity and hear the truth of His word. The time has come to let go of what you have always been doing and ask the hard questions to determine if it is still the right thing to do. It is time to truly let God touch every area and let Him guide you through the things that need adjusting. This era is no longer the time of "it has worked thus far," "that is what I have always done," "my pastor says this is the way," or "my momma/daddy/cousin says this is correct."

Your journey and relationship with God does not belong to others; it is time to take ownership of your walk. Too often, we stay complacent because human beings are creatures of habit and comfort. However, habit can leave us stuck and stagnated. Change can be hard, but the ability to not change in this area will be a great hindrance in your life and your ability to walk in freedom. Grace is always with us, but grace shifts as we know better. It is not an excuse to stay stuck and avoid accountability, responsibility, and ownership. Grace is a place to grow.

In the natural, our children use diapers until they can use the restroom on their own. Once they have mastered the restroom, the grace for wearing pampers has worn off. Grace transcends and transitions as we grow in maturity. Believers, the time has come for the Body to transition from borrower to lender so that we can be the change agent of the world that God is calling us to be. My declaration for each of you is that God gives you a swift financial revelation for your life. I speak freedom, clarity, and truth in every area of your life.

The purpose of this book is not to discourage people from giving. Giving is still required. Some of you reading this book will be Kingdom financiers, funding many exploits in the Kingdom of God.

Remember and carry this prophetic word as well as the previous one: "God will never put on you what the cross took off you. This is your assurance and the blessing that you can lay hold of," says the Father. I am trusting God that this is His truth and that it will be a source of hope, a catalyst for change, and an eye-opening revelation for those who are eager to follow the word of the Lord.

A Sneak Peak: The Kingdom Strategy of God

The following is an excerpt from the next book of this series. This book will cover the details of Kingdom Economics and the restoration of Kingdom finances. It is a guide for us to begin operating the way that God desires, which is us functioning as lenders and not borrowers as well as removing our dependency on the world system.

Two terms need to be introduced in this book for understanding the direction that the Body of Christ should move toward in the future concerning giving. The first term is *authorized giving.* Authorized givers are the ones who are simply in a financial state to give without it disrupting the basic needs of life. Giving should not be a burden. Giving should be cheerful and not stressful. It is one thing to forgo Starbucks, Netflix, or some other non-essential need to be a giver in the Kingdom of God. Abraham and Jacob cannot be used to support tithing, but they can be used as examples to show who should be supporting the Kingdom as well as how. They gave out of their increase. Abraham gave a tenth of the spoils of war. Jacob asked God to increase him and he promised to return a tenth to God as a result. That was a respective covenant (promise) between them and God.

Unauthorized givers are not in a position to give and should not be shamed, manipulated, or otherwise placed in a position to keep them in a struggling state. If a single parent is struggling to feed the family and has to decide between feeding her family or paying tithes (or even giving), there is no choice. They should take care of their family. They should not give and be told to trust God. No! Let the leaders of the church lead by example and trust God. That is a key part of the plan that God has designed for moving forward. The church always tells its members to trust God, but this is an opportunity to practice what they preach. The church has to focus on teaching people how to hear the Holy Spirit and let Him convict and resign their position of trying to be the Holy Spirit in the lives of their members.

Giving should not be used as a bargaining tool, criteria, or requirement for serving in the church. The concept for authorized and unauthorized givers is addressed in Galatians 3:20-24:

"Now a mediator is not a mediator of one, but God is one. Is the law then against the promises of God? God forbid: for if there had been a law given which could have given life, verily righteousness should have been by the law. But the scripture hath concluded all under sin, that the promise by faith of Jesus Christ might be given to them that believe. But before faith came, we were kept under the law, shut up unto the faith which should afterwards be revealed. Wherefore the law was our schoolmaster to bring us unto Christ, that we might be justified by faith."

The scripture is clear that we should give cheerfully. 2 Corinthians 9:7 states that, "Every man according as he purposeth in his heart, so let him give; not grudgingly, or of necessity: for God loveth a cheerful giver." No one can give cheerfully if they are only giving not to be cursed. Sometimes unauthorized financial givers can serve in other ways, but are made to feel less than because of the size of their bank account.

Luke 6:38 states, "Give, and it shall be given unto you; good measure, pressed down, and shaken together, and running over, shall men give into your bosom. For with the same measure that ye mete withal it shall be measured to you again." This scripture isn't just about money; it is about giving in your everyday life. The Message version of this scripture states, "Don't pick on people, jump on their failures, criticize their faults – unless, of course, you want the same treatment. Don't condemn those who are down; that hardness can boomerang. Be easy on people; you'll find life a lot easier. Give away your life; you'll find life given back, but not merely given back – given back with bonus and blessing. Giving, not getting, is the way. Generosity begets generosity."

Your time, your talents, and your gifts are ways of giving. Simply put, we give because we love Him.

References

Blizzard, Roy Dr. *Tithing Giving and Prosperity.* Bible Scholars, Inc ISBN: 13:978-1484087619. 2013

Blog. www.theoldchurch.blogspot.com. I'm Going To Pay My Tithe First Says Evander Holyfield. 26 April 2009

Eberhardt-Starks, Cheryl. Biblical Teacher and Prophet. Personal Interview. 2017

Hayes Press. Bible Covenants 101. Hayes Press Publisher Resources and Media. 2015

Connecting with LaQuetta

LaQuetta Holyfield Glaze is the published author of "The Art of the Journey: The Reboot," written to help others discover God in everyday life. A Coach. A Pioneer. A Motivator. A Spiritual Guide. Her life passion is to nurture others into their greater purpose and life outside the limits of their imagination. She encourages people to go into deeper relationships with God by teaching them how to see His presence in everyday living. Her life mission is to comfort the disturbed and to disturb the comfortable.

Getting Social with LaQuetta

Facebook: www.facebook.com/KingdomPioneerInstitute

Instagram: www.instagram.com/kingdompioneers

To book LaQuetta for speaking engagements, coaching (author, life, leadership, spiritual and executive) please contact us via email: laquettag@kingdompioneerinstitute.com.

www.ingramcontent.com/pod-product-compliance
Lightning Source LLC
Chambersburg PA
CBHW070438010526
44118CB00014B/2100